Table of Contents

Introduction

How would you like to have the ultimate power of control over other people? It sounds good, doesn't it? Well, we'll tell you up front, this book will share with you the secrets of powerful people from every walk of life. From politicians to CEOs to religious leaders to celebrities, all of these people use the methods and techniques we will lay out here. Not only will these prove to be extremely powerful, but they are secrets anyone can master. Let us assure you: There is no one who is not capable of mastering these techniques.

So why is it not more common? Well, they actually are somewhat common, but not everybody knows all of them or how to make use of them. Even low-level salesmen or the hustler at the corner market is savvy enough to use some variety of psychological tactics. For the rest,

The Art of Psychological Warfare

How to Skillfully Influence People Undetected and How to Mentally Subdue Your Enemies in Stealth Mode

By Michael T. Steven

many people are afraid of having this much power. They're afraid that using these techniques makes you a sociopath, a schemer, or a hypocrite.

We'll say right up front: You can abuse psychological warfare to your own profit and advantage. We leave it up to you to make your moral decisions of whether to use these tactics for good or ill. Just because you learn how to steal cars doesn't mean you should go around stealing cars; you can use that knowledge to prevent car theft as well. In "hacker" circles, this book would be considered a manual on "social engineering," because basically this is a manual for hacking other people's brains. But you have to remember that hackers work for the police and the government too. And as we'll find out, police and governments use social engineering too!

As you read through this book, keep in mind that the following traits will be beneficial to you when you try to put this book into practice:

- **Confidence** - In today's society, this is almost a taboo word by itself. For those of you who don't feel confident, just fake it. We will dwell on confidence many times in this work. For now, we'll just say "Act like a winner and the world will treat you like one."

- **Appearance** - Your social standing with other people maxes out depending on how good you look. If nature made you ugly, do the best with what you have. At the very least, good hygiene and well-kept clothes will get you far.

- **Temperance** - This is the wisdom to know how to pick your battles and when it's worth moving in as opposed to when to back out. It will keep you out of trouble.

- **A sense of humor** - Funny people make other people laugh, when you laugh you feel good, and when somebody makes you feel good, you trust them more. At the least, a sense of humor will help you make light of it when you fail.

How to read this book

Psychological warfare is a highly specialized topic requiring advanced knowledge of psychology. We will provide some science, some history, and some examples along with more specific how-to instructions. It is recommended that you seek outside research of topics where we mention that there's much more to a topic (e.g. neuro-linguistic programming) that space and time prevented us from providing.

At the end of each section where relevant, you'll find a bulleted list of tips on using the information in that chapter to apply to your own conflicts in life. It is advised that you digest everything and not just head for the bullet-points, however. Using psychology to influence people and mentally subdue enemies is a deep art.

Chapter 1: History of Psychological Warfare

Just how potent is psychological warfare? How much can you do to another person without laying a single finger on them? Here are a few examples to illustrate what a tremendous power this is to wield.

From the years 1959 to 1962, Henry Alexander Murray, while director of the Psychological Clinic, participated in the CIA's Project MKUltra. These were brutal psychological experiments intended to measure test subjects under stress. But one test stands out in history.

In the test, volunteer university students had to write an essay which summarized their philosophy on life and things they believed in. They would then be sent to a debate room where they were led to expect that they'd discuss their ideas with another student like themselves. Instead, however, they would encounter a trained interrogator, whose job was to use the students' own beliefs to attack and belittle them, browbeating them out of every core virtue they thought was right in the world. Since the whole experiment had the purpose of putting the student through as much stress as possible, students came out of the experience rattled and traumatized.

One of these students was named Ted Kaczynski, a 17-year-old prodigy who had already made an impression in the field of advanced mathematical research. But history knows this student better by the assumed alias he took on after being discouraged from academia and ultimately resigning. Ted Kaczynski went on to become the Unabomber, a serial killer who waged a terrorist campaign of mail-bombs against universities from the years 1978 to 1995, before finally being captured.

We will talk more about Project MKUltra later, because it's fundamental to the study of psychological warfare.

For a defensive example, in 2005, British actor Benedict Cumberbatch found himself ensnared in a real-life crisis that resembled a scene from one of his own movies. While in South Africa shooting a film, a car he was riding in blew a flat on a desolate road and he was attacked by a gang of armed thieves in the virtually lawless outland. They kidnapped him. But he talked his way out of it.

First he feigned a heart condition to avoid being tied up and stuffed into the car trunk. Then he persuaded them, as a notable British actor, that he was worth almost nothing as a hostage, but if they harmed him, the news would spark international headlines that would lead to war. The kidnappers dropped him off in a nearby village unharmed and sped away. That's what you call acting for your life!

As one might guess, acting lends a lot of skills to psychological warfare.

Italian Renaissance author Niccolo Machiavelli was a famous proponent and codifier for many psychological warfare techniques. So much so that he lends his name to the term "Machiavellianism," the use of cunning and duplicity in conducting business. Basically every corrupt politician has read a page or two out of Machiavelli's work "The Prince."

Machiavelli's philosophies continue to be the base for a whole body of business literature. Modern day business books teach how to maintain power, behave in manipulating ways, and use harsh management decisions that are nevertheless good for the bottom line. One may well argue, in American corporate capitalism, that when we create a business and grant it the same rights as a human (what 'incorporating' means), while not holding it to any moral restrictions except for "survive at all costs and make your shareholders rich," what you have effectively created is an institutionalized psychopath.

We will be using many more lessons from the business world in this book.

On March the 15th, 1783, none the less than George Washington pulled off a brilliant coup of psychological warfare. The event is known in history books as the Newburgh address. The Newburgh conspiracy was a mob of officers in the Continental Army, whose aims were to start a military rebellion against the then-new United States Congress. In a meeting held to appease the rebels and attempt to forestall the movement, Washington was not scheduled to speak, but showed up. The astonished intended speaker relinquished the podium to Washington, and he took the stage in front of the armed and unruly mob of rebels.

What matters here is not so much the text of the address itself, but Washington's clever trick before the address. Fumbling in his pocket for his spectacles, he said, "Gentlemen, you will permit me to put on my spectacles, for I have not only grown gray but almost blind in the service of my country." This caused the men to understand that the legend before them had suffered and sacrificed far greater than they had. The realization stung and disheartened the rebels, many of whom threw down their weapons and left in tears of shame on the spot.

The address itself is a matter of public record. But it's just an example here of how a forefather of a nation can use psychological warfare to impressive results!

Some of the ideas in this book may seem controversial. Well, of course they are! All strange ideas are shocking. And all new ideas are strange. That's why they're new, because you've never encountered them before. Go ahead and try to do anything completely original and not have it come out shocking. It has nothing to do with the ideas; it has everything to do with novelty.

We will be studying many more of the lessons in history. For now, let's move on to the lesson so we can discover how to use this power ourselves. In using psychological warfare tactics, the most important thing is to understand psychology itself. This takes some patience, and we will try to liven up the following two chapters to make it as painless and brief as possible. Do not skip over it, however. It is the foundation, without which the rest of this book would crumble.

Take-aways:

- Appreciate that you have a lot to learn.
- Develop an attitude of respect towards this art.
- Don't use it lightly.

Chapter 2: How To Read People

Ironically enough, the very thing that will make you better at psychological warfare is also the first thing that gives you a good defense against it. While an in-depth education in psychology is impossible for this book - you'd want a university degree to go with it - parts of it are necessary to our topic, and they all start with reading people.

Reading people is important because you're in the business of trying to manipulate them, power struggle with them, and mentally dominate them. Watching for "tells" and indicators can tell you what's working and what isn't, where a person's weaknesses are, or what may lead you to a truce.

Did we say "truce"? Make no mistake about it right now: Even though our subject is psychological warfare, if your target gives into you, you win anyway. It's a big win to be able to mentally dominate someone and have them not even aware it was happening. If they concede to you, negotiate with you, or offer to work with you towards a compromise - that's a win. This isn't about a power trip, it's about getting what you want.

Body Language

Body language is the non-verbal communications that all humans do, whether they're aware of it or not. For our purposes, it is important to know not just to read other people, but to control your own body language to have the desired effect.

If you have a hard time getting a grasp on body language, find a friend with a dog. Dogs are an excellent education in body language, because they are very expressive and relate to humans, but also can't talk themselves. A dog who wants to go out with their master for outdoor exercise will frolic and bounce around, showing what fun they're going to have. An aggressive dog will bristle and stand erect, snarling and crouching to pounce, as it barks at the mailman - this is warning that it's going to attack. A dog who just accidentally knocked a vase over, which broke, will hang its head and look at its master sheepishly, showing it is ashamed for its error.

For another example of non-human expressive body language, look at animated cartoons such as Tom & Jerry. The two characters have no dialogue at all, yet manage to convey to the audience all kinds of thoughts, reactions, and goals as they scamper about on their misadventures. Analyzing the pantomime of silent characters in animation gives you a real appreciation for what a fine art it actually is. At the same time, consider that this is entertainment fare intended for young children, which goes to show just how intuitive body language is to communication.

The goals in studying body language for psychological warfare should be:

- Recognizing when your opponent is resistant to you or defiant of you.
- Seeing when a person is vulnerable.
- Spotting fear and anxiety.
- Exploiting signals sent by your target.
- Adjusting your own body language and posture strategically.

A full list of examples of every kind of body language is beyond this book's scope - there are whole books on this subject. Instead, we'll provide some examples:

- **Adjusting glasses** - This is a sign that a person is skeptical or is paying more attention.
- **Preening** - A person putting on a display for the opposite sex. There's a whole vocabulary here; women twirl their hair, bite their lip, and swagger their hips when they walk, while men stride with their head high, flex their muscles, throw out their chest, and hold their head up confidently.

One noted macho pose is the "Captain Morgan pose," the same as on the bottle of rum. Knee cocked, foot up and resting on some prop, with the rest of the body straight and the chest out, head back, in a state of relaxed confidence. It's a territorial pose; it says "I've conquered this place or challenge and emerged the victor. Address me as a hero."

- **Facepalm** - Popular on the Internet. Clapping a hand to your face near the eyes is the universal expression for "That was so stupid I can't believe it!"
- Finger on the lips - As any librarian can tell you, this means "Shh, be quiet." Any gesture towards the mouth can mean "don't speak" or "speak softly." When people have to stop and think about what to say, they also put a thoughtful hand over their mouth.

People who are telling a lie also tend to put a hand towards their mouth. It's as if they were trying to fix what they were saying as it came out, or disguise their speech as if they were saying "this isn't the real me talking."

- **Rubbing the back of the head or neck** - This can be a nervous gesture to fake nonchalance. It's a subtle grooming signal. "What, is something wrong here? Nothing's wrong!" Generally there are many movements involving the hands and the head that should be a tell that the subject is not being truthful in some way or another. Anything that's played like a burst of nervous energy or fidgeting is suspect.

- **Looking away** - Averting the eye's gaze is the classic gesture of "I don't like that." Kids being attacked by the school bully look down. Witnesses to a car accident flick their head away when they catch view of a bloody victim. A person who has decided not to buy an item stops looking at it. A kid refusing to eat his vegetables turns his nose up to the ceiling. If you roll your eyes at what someone says, it's the universal sign for "I think you're crazy."

Eye contact is so important, both giving and receiving, that we'll delve more into it later.

- **Slouching** - Either standing with a relaxed pose or sprawling all over the furniture, this shows a person who is aloof, casual, and not at all alert or vigilant.
- **Nose tapping with a finger** - "I know something you don't."
- **Hand on the cheek** - This is a subconscious gesture that says "I'm bored" or "I'm tired." Especially exaggerated by tilting the head sideways. The person is miming "I'm ready for bed, see, this is my head on the pillow."
- **Head tilted by itself** - This is the universal gesture for "That's strange!" Something you're never seen before, just realizing something that's off about a situation, intrigued, perplexed, or otherwise unusual. It's so characteristic that even animals do it. It's a reflex where you're encountering an

unfamiliar object and getting a different angle view of it.

- **Crossed arms** - The universal symbol for "I'm not accepting this." The person has stopped listening to you, is planning on putting up a fight to resist you, or is skeptical of you.

This is just a small sample of the vocabulary of body language. While not all of it is important to you, developing an awareness of it will work to your benefit. The whole world can be conquered by the person who pays more attention than everybody else.

Take-aways:

- Use body language to size up your opponent.
- Adjust your own body language to influence your opponent.
- Keep an awareness of your opponent's reacts and body language vocabulary while interacting with them.

- Use your awareness of body language to subtly influence any conversation.

Cold Reading

The term "cold reading" actually comes from the world of those who attempt or fake psychic powers - hypnotists, fortune tellers, and stage magicians. Like body language, cold reading is a set of observations you can make which will tell you things about a subject without so much as engaging them in conversation.

While you're learning all this fun stuff, you might as well treat yourself to a few party tricks. Here's a sample "script" for being a stage psychic:

Walk out in front of an audience of about 900 people in a studio. Start by explaining that the visions you receive might make more sense to the spectators than to you, so if they can help you out by responding to your cues, you can unravel some answers together.

You want the audience eager to pounce on anything you say and develop it into a narrative.

Now start with "Who's Betty?" In a room full of 900 people, you might have a Betty. If not, each of them knows an average of about 150 people, so you're sure to hit a Betty in there somewhere. Watch the reactions. Anybody who reacts is either Betty or knows Betty. They'll tell you.

They knew a Betty? You have a vision of a Betty in the past. Was she close to you? Well, of course, Betty was probably the subject's aunt, sister, mother, etc. Keep saying these until they stop you. Oh, it turns out Betty is their long-lost great aunt.

Keep prompting them until they babble the nature of their relationship to Betty. Yes, she died of breast cancer in the 1990s, so the target knew Betty when they were very young. So did you visit Betty when you were a child? Yes, every summer in Cape Cod. Well, Betty has a message of comfort to you from beyond the grave, that she loved you very much, and I'm getting... something red. The target will immediately jump to a red dress, red toy wagon, red car... Say something about the car as a fond memory or whatever. The target will mix up the events in their head and go home telling everybody this amazing psychic talked to the ghost of her great-aunt Betty, even knew about the red rocking horse in her living room!

Other prompts include: "I see a male figure, a father figure in the past, someone who you had a quarrel with but wants you to know they loved you anyway." Or "I sense a woman with blackness in her chest, like she had heart disease." This will apply to at least half the people at a random sample, and somebody will obligingly jump up and yell "I know who you're talking about!"

The above script doesn't just happen by itself, though. When you start throwing out there cues, they're probes with a statistically probably chance of being true. Once somebody latches onto this, you offer more guiding cues to narrow the perceived event down. The subject will have various reactions which you observe carefully and use to tell when you're on the right path.

Here's the clip-n-save:

- People who look up are remembering a true event or recalling a fact.
- People who look off to the side or down are picturing something that didn't happen or considering something that isn't true.
- Some people - but not all - show other patterns of eye behavior, such as glancing to the left when thinking of the past and to the right when they think about the future.

Cold reading is a subset of what we call the "Barnum effect." Named after circus tycoon P. T. Barnum, it's where you make a general, hazy statement that could apply to almost anyone that someone will personalize as if it were specific to them. For instance, here is your horoscope:

"You have a need to be well-liked and popular, but you can also be very shy. While you are critical of yourself sometimes, you also have untapped capacity which you could take advantage of. You sometimes doubt whether you have made the right decision. You pride yourself as an independent thinker and insist on proof of claims you're skeptical about. You have recently experienced the death of a loved one, and a moderate sum of money and a short, but memorable, trip is in your future."

Spot on, wasn't it?

It applies to everybody, though.

Another version of cold reading is the famed "palm reading" trick. The trick is that you hold their hand in yours, but hold it very lightly, because their hand is going to move around and tell you stuff subconsciously. When you tell them good news, or something that's true, they'll open up their hand

wider and lift it towards your face. "Tell me more!"
Tell them bad news or something that isn't true, and
they'll curl their hand up and tug it back. "I've heard
enough."

Understanding cold reading means understanding
the commonality of human existence and the
experiences we all share. Knowing this will be
applicable in your quest to master psychological
warfare. When you're interacting with people, read
their body language, eye cues, facial expression, and
the tone of their voice. Look for signs that they're
nervous, optimistic, critical, etc., and then ask
yourself why they are feeling this way.

For yet another example of psychological tricks
involving metaphysical mumbo-jumbo, we
interviewed a local psychology expert who agreed to
disclose the following:

"When I was working my way through college with
random odd jobs, I fell in with some

charlatans who ran a New-Age shop full of love potions and Tarot cards. I was fascinated by the psychology behind it. Soon I learned some of the tricks you use to bamboozle people.

The number-one thing you have to know is: People want to be fooled. Anybody who walks into a psychic booth is already convinced themselves that you're for real; you just have to play into their fantasy.

Prompting is your best trick. All you have to say is something like "I sense that someone in your life has passed away recently." Statistically, you're spot on. They'll suddenly babble about their dead uncle Harry and tell you all sorts of stuff you never would have guessed. Now say "I can see very clearly one particular memory of your uncle Harry - I see the color red!" Oh, Harry wore red pants one time or drove a red car or had a cat with a red collar. Later they'll tell their friends that you "knew" about their uncle Harry - even what color car he drove! Without their telling you anything! Amazing!

And the best is the power of suggestion. We had these crystals we'd sell. It's as simple as holding up a crystal to their hand and babbling that you're going to charge your energy field through their chakra, "tell me when you feel anything". Well, duh, they're participating in this silly ritual, of course they're going to will themselves into thinking that their hand is getting warm, or you're pinching their cuticle, or you're channeling the hand of their dead great-grandfather.

It's all blathering nonsense. There's nothing here more sophisticated than the skill set of the average prostitute. They want a fantasy - you supply it. You can do this half-asleep.

You can think of it like poker. In poker, you watch your opponent for tells, these little body-language clues that say what the person is thinking. Just make a broad, general statement, then let the subject's tells lead you to the specific details."

This is a rare skill in our day and age because we live in an age of limited face-to-face contact and interaction. Electronic communications have replaced most of our human interaction. The lack of practice dulls our edge when it comes to relating to people on a real level. Which means being just a little bit good at it is like having a superpower.

Reading techniques filter into using psychological manipulation, but there's much more to consider yet.

Take-aways:

- Use cold reading on people to "read their mind." The more you know that they don't say out loud, the more advantage you have.
- Use the Barnum effect to make general statements about the person you want to influence, but they will take as personally significant to them.
- Use people's willingness to be fooled to subtly persuade them into doing your bidding.

- Impress people you want to influence with your uncanny reading skills - it's like casting a spell on some people!

Culture and Class

IMPORTANT NOTE: Going forward, we'll have to say somewhere in here that if you're offended by any of our points debunking something you believe in... well, you'll just have to live with it. You can not be an effective psychological combatant and still cherish beliefs in hard religion, pseudo-science, or superstitions. Belief in these things make your targets more vulnerable; you should be exploiting them, not falling for them yourself.

The assumptions you make when you're reading people will change depending on who you're dealing with. People from different backgrounds have different frames of reference.

You'll notice, for example, that phony psychics and religious faith-healers tend to prey on the lower classes. The same goes for cheap superstitions and get-rich-quick scams. Look over the selection of supermarket tabloids and notice how they appeal to the seedy interests and bread-and-circuses.

People from lower-class backgrounds tend to fall for this kind of thing more often. That's because people with an upper-class background are more likely to have a college education and perhaps even a university degree. This at least gives them exposure to skeptical thinking, debate skills, and a bit of learning.

Detectives have a technique they call the "Sherlock Scan," where you look somebody up and down and try to read as much as possible about their station in life. If you're dealing with somebody in a three-piece suit and tie, with an expensive watch and top-grade shoes, you can be reasonably sure you're talking to a professional with a degree and six-figure salary career. By the same token, a man with greasy hands and a stained blue jumpsuit is probably an engineer or auto mechanic. It's easy to do, right?

This is common sense stuff, but you can take it to the next step by trying to put yourself into the other person's place. You can be more persuasive by appealing to a person's interests and values. A stay-at-home mother of five children will have a different set of values from a New York lawyer; A corporate CEO will have different interests and values from an inner-city drug dealer.

While we're doing disclaimers, here's another one: If you tend to discriminate against people for reasons of race, gender, orientation, or creed, now's the time to drop that too. Holding onto bigoted beliefs will only cloud your judgment when reading people. Furthermore, your dislike of a person just for their skin color or sexual orientation will be something that person can pick up, unnecessarily putting people on the defensive. When you deal in psychological warfare, your only concern should be winning - without pride or prejudice.

As an exercise, practice sizing people up wherever you go. Put together your knowledge of cold reading, body language, and assessing people's background to work, getting a fix on people you see every day.

The most important thing to remember about people everywhere, though, is that they just want to belong. In fact, this is the default setting for all of humanity. Every subculture, without exception, has people in it just to be "cool" and they make up the majority. Religion, politics, philosophy, heroin usage, having kids, punk rock, bikers, BDSM, hackers, geeks, hipsters, furries, professors. People live their whole lives to please other people because they're terrified paralyzed by not having the approval of others.

This is why "peer pressure" works. This is where the expression "monkey see monkey do" comes from. This is why religions are so hard to suppress. This is why they sell bumper stickers and T-shirts. Who should seriously care that your child was an honor student?

This is why they market beverages with an image conveyed by the product instead of the aspects of the product itself. Do they say "Buy Mountain Dew, it tastes better and has more caffeine and sugar to give you extra energy"? No, they market it with extreme sports people jumping dirt bikes off mountains and parachuting off bridges. Look how cool these people are! Drink this and you'll be cool too.

This is why kids will beg their mommies to buy junk cereal with a cartoon character on the box and not care how it tastes.

This is why people have a mid-life crisis at age 40. They went to school to get a degree and start a career in a profession they never wanted, just because their parents pressured them.

This is why arranged marriages happen. This is why there are closeted gays who are married just for appearances' sake.

This drives the majority of human social interaction, business, culture, and politics.

Oh, and those like buttons on Facebook? You know why you feel that little thrill when they boost your score? You just experience peer approval and class validation. And that makes us all happy monkeys.

Take-aways:

- Use your awareness of what we have in common to understand your opponent.
- Put your observation skills of human behavior together with body language and cold reading to gain a better understanding of your opponent's personality.

Empathy

Rounding out our course in reading your target, there is the matter of empathy. Empathy is the ability to understand what another person is experiencing from their point of view. We've been leading up to this throughout the book so far.

Empathy can help you determine when your target is feeling weak and caving in, or bold and confident. Empathy is the creative portion of psychological combat. It takes an act of applied imagination to see somebody argue with their wife, then go out and kick their car, and be able to understand that they're actually angry with their wife and not their car.

Empathy is also a highly developed skill. If you're born with it, you're blessed, but if not, you have to work to earn it. Our upcoming chapters will help you out with learning empathy, but if you're not good with it, you might not be the best psychological warrior in the world. Some people are just born being cold fish and there's not much they can do about it.

But assuming you're not affected with an autism spectrum disorder, there is hope for you.

Take-aways:

- Develop your skills of reading people via body language, cold reading, and scanning external clues for background and culture.
- Develop your empathy. It's a powerful skill, since saying the right words to touch people deeply at the right time can catch them off-guard and open them up to you.

Why people are the way they are

Why can't we solve all of our problems together and live in peace and harmony?

There are no justified answers to that question. But there are off-the-hip theories, and all you need is one that works at the moment.

Not only have we evolved from lesser beings, we may have just barely begun to evolve and it will be millions of years before we can accomplish what we hope to achieve. Unfortunately, here we are stuck in the present. This means that everybody alive to read this is leading an almost completely pointless life. We're animals. We can try to attain immortality through our work, but 99% of everything worth preserving just ends up trampled into the dirt by the successive generations of animals.

Most of the problems humans have are unsolvable, because we will not work together. At least, not without putting our own selfish interests first.

Millions of years from now, after we're farther down the evolutionary tree, we might be ready to work together to solve our problems then. But by that time, virtually everything we know now will be hazy myths by then, occasionally excavated by archaeologists but cast aside in puzzlement.

The only thing we can do is try to build bridges between those few who have some sense, working towards making the way ready for our successors to begin trying to solve humanity's problems as soon as possible. Think of it as a "jump start" strategy. It may not work, but it has the greatest chance of being useful of any other strategy we can think of.

We're just apes. We didn't evolve from apes; we ARE apes. Even our greatest members are barely better than the worst of us. Fortunately, we have the optimism of a vastly improved future for humanity, to save us from total despair. We have seen tiny bits of progress in the last couple of centuries. Landing on the moon, inventing computers, doubling our natural lifespan. They seem like vast, magnificent achievements to us. Yes, and a dog thinks that he is very clever for knowing how to fetch a ball, too.

As we look back on the Stone Age as a time of primitive savagery, so are we - even our top achievers - primitive savages in the view of the future, TRULY civilized human looking back at us. In fact, perhaps the first step towards that progressive future is to realize that, as a species, we are too immature to progress yet.

NOTE: Do not mistake this for nihilism. This does not mean that we should wreck suffering and madness because "hey, why not?" That's actually a symptom of our savage nature. We should still conduct ourselves in the fashion that will make Earth the greatest paradise we are capable of, so that, again, our future evolved selves get that "jump start." Just because we're still animals doesn't mean we can't be happy animals.

There, that's as cosmic as we can get. But for your day to day answers and the purposes of this book, it's a workable philosophy.

Take-aways:

- Just have a bit of philosophy on hand to help you frame your interactions with people.
- Know when a person is responding as a person, and when it's the pre-evolved monkey talking. Instinctive, emotional responses are the primal ones.

Chapter 3: How To Be Likable

Our last chapter taught us about how to size up your intended targets. In this chapter, we'll talk about how to likewise look at how you present yourself.

Why should you care how you seem to other people? Because in psychological warfare, we leave no path to victory un-taken. If you triumph because your target thinks you're kind of cute, that's a victory. If your target knows that you're being manipulative but gives in to you anyway because they're out of patience, that's a victory. If your target knows you're conning them but they're not going to do anything about it because you're intimidating them, that's a victory. The best combat of all was the one where one of the participants had no idea that they were in combat.

Presenting yourself to other people is tremendously important. You're attempting social engineering, after all, so all you have to bring is yourself. You need the best version of yourself you can muster together.

Socialization

Over and over, we hear about the stereotype of the modern-day socially isolated person. They're not good with people. They don't know how to make friends. They have trouble talking to strangers. They don't get out much.

What is the problem here? Modern day society in Western culture just seems to foster people with a bend for Asperger's syndrome. Tech careers are in demand, resulting in people who spend more time dealing with machines than people. Families are smaller, so there are fewer siblings to interact with and fewer elders to talk to. Single parent families mean the one parent is working full-time to make ends meet. And of course, the electronic devices we all find so handy also interfere with our people skills. Many of us are more comfortable interacting over the Internet than in person.

There are easy ways to become socialized, but they all have something in common: You have to get out more!

Mission #1: Join a club, group, or organization. No matter what the focus of these groups are, all clubs are "social" clubs. Find a hobby, interest or pursuit and a group associated with it and join it. The ideal is the kind of group that meets once a week at a public place. Go there and make friends. Aggressively! Find other people hanging out at the fringes being shy and bring them into the warmth. Offer to help out with activities.

Avoid places like bars and clubs. These are stereotypical places people go to socialize, but actually they're just traps to spend money while you get drunk, with the music up way too loud to have a conversation.

Mission #2: Volunteer! Find a local charity and donate your time. This is solid social gold in so many ways, it's a wonder more people don't do it. Haven't you ever noticed that a person who selflessly helps others immediately has their attractiveness doubled? Pack lunches for the homeless, mop up a shelter, collect donations for research to fight a disease, visit a rest home. Support your local library. Or get politically involved and canvass for your favorite candidate. Volunteering looks great on your resume, gives you a positive sense of purpose in the world, and gets you out and socializing all at the same time. Your fellow volunteers will be great connections for later networking, and the experience will make you a broader, more well-rounded person.

Take-aways:

- Develop and cultivate your social skills. You can never have enough!
- Use your social skills in influencing and mentally subduing targets.
- Use everything you learn about human interaction to your benefit in interacting with people.

Charisma

What is it that makes some people an instant social magnet? They're the life of the party and a driving force at work. They're natural born leaders; they have to only speak up and the entire room turns to listen to them. They have such power over everyone else! How do we get to be that popular?

This again, is an art, which is finely practiced. Here are some tips to work on your charisma, and you can put them all into practice which you're busy getting socialized with all the suggestions above.

- **SMILE!** That's the number one tip for charisma. It doesn't matter if inside, you are a shriveled ball of misery and angst, never show that to the world. Fake it until you feel it. Be the ray of sunshine and everybody will gravitate to you.

- **Don't take yourself seriously!** At least, don't act like you do. Be relaxed and casual about yourself; project the image that you're "just trying to get by."

- **Never criticize others.** Unless it feeds directly into a current point of tactical warfare, be the kind of person who follows the golden rule "If you can't say something nice, don't say anything at all." Especially be careful not to be caught gossiping - when you tell Alice you think Bob is cheating, that just makes Alice wonder what you say about her when she's not around.

- **Speak glowingly of others.**
  Compliments cost you nothing, and yet
  people are so stingy with them, you'd
  think they had to sign them in blood or
  something. Hand them out like candy. If
  you like what somebody does, has, or
  says, say so. It's really very simple: If you
  make people feel better, they will like you.

- **Give other people your full
  attention.** Nothing is so flattering than
  to be the undivided focus of attention.
  This means put away your phone, don't
  constantly glance at your watch or your
  computer monitor, don't scan the horizon
  like you're waiting for a stampede to come
  over the hill. Look at the person you're
  talking to.

- **Listen twice as much as you speak.**
  After smiling, this is the number two
  simplest and most effective rule. When
  you listen, you should be fully focused on
  the other person and not just waiting for
  your turn to talk. Some people listen to

other people talk like they're waiting in a car for a red light to change.

Between the socializing and the charisma, it sounds like this is a book on how to be popular in high school. But we have to assure you, this is about psychological warfare. You have the advantage if you're a well-socialized person with great charisma.

Also, don't belittle high school. Lots of people never move on from high school mentally, and we're sure you can think of several examples you know already.

Take-aways:

- Develop your charisma to make yourself a naturally charming and influential person.
- Use your charisma to subdue potential enemies, converting them into friends.

Disarming Defenses

One last tip for winning psychological combat is how to make yourself appear less threatening, and easier to get along with.

If you're any good at psychological tactics, chances are that you're a bold and confident person. And if you're not confident? Gotta work on that.

To be confident, be capable. Live out loud. Get in adventures, get lost, get found again, live your life instead of letting it happen to you like a reality show. Allow no challenge to go unconquered. CARE about how things are going to go, and then bust your ass to make them go your way. After a few years of this, there's no challenge you can face where you can't say "Well, I survived that other time, so I'll survive this too!"

Be a lion and not a mouse. Don't be mean, be noble, but still be a lion. One of these times you're going to stand your ground against something badder than you and it'll kill you, but you'll die with no regrets then because your life was a life lived out loud.

But some people are just plain intimidated by bold, confident people. The thing you have to realize is that the human race, by and large, is characterized by fear. Most political conflict revolves around fear. We build walls and fences to keep each other out, from fear. We fear social isolation, financial failure, our own declining health, and dying alone. Wars are nothing but fears playing out.

You have to assume everyone you talk to is a scared and timid bunny rabbit until proven otherwise. So this is a section on making people trust you.

- **Dress for success.** It doesn't matter if you don't have a million-dollar budget for expensive clothes. This is more about being neat and tidy, and well-groomed. Taking care of yourself will help others care more about you too. There is also the very true adage that if you dress like a winner, the world will treat you like one. The difference is in how people treat you. Combine being well-dressed and well-groomed with a vague air of authority and a lot of confidence, and people will let you do anything! Go backstage, invade the stockroom, barge right down hospital corridors, march right into the command center like you own the place. You can bark orders at people and they obey them without thinking. You can just take charge everywhere.

- **Have a sense of humor.** Nothing is more disarming than a good laugh. When public speakers begin to take the podium, they lead off with a joke or funny anecdote. It doesn't matter if you're not a natural comedian. Anybody can make a flip remark or a simple pun. You can't laugh without smiling, so at least getting people to smile, however weakly, makes them that much more open to you.

- **Again, don't take yourself too seriously.** While you're working on your sense of humor, make yourself the butt of the joke at least 50% of the time. Self-deprecating humor works on many levels: It makes people laugh, it shows them that you're not a narcissist, and it gets them on your side defending you even before they know they're doing it. Mind you, don't be negatively self-critical. Make yourself seem like "one of the regular people," not lower.

This just about rounds up our examination of people skills that help with psychological warfare. If you glossed over this chapter wanting to get to the "good stuff," go back and read it, because that is the good stuff! People have achieved fame, fortune, and celebrity using nothing but the advice in this chapter.

But coming up next, our first actual weapon: Persuasion.

Take-aways:

- Work on your confidence, to make yourself a stronger influencer.
- Be subtle (as in 'stealth mode') by making yourself seem to not be a threat. This will both psychologically disarm enemies and make people you want to influence trust you more.

Chapter 4: Getting People To Agree With You

Convincing other people to agree with you is the ultimate in psychological domination. You have successfully imposed your will on another mind. No matter how minor it is, every time you do this, you should note it as a little victory. Because it's practice for the bigger challenges, and because it will help you build confidence.

When you're working in the art of persuasion, you should work to always mount your confidence. A shy, retiring, complacent debater isn't very convincing. In the following tips in this chapter, work on having confidence when you practice them - but make sure it's real confidence, and not just false braggadocio. Being bullying or condescending will turn your target off. Instead, you should phrase everything with an attitude that what you're advocating is the most right thing in the world, and your arguments are a friendly invitation to help the other person join you in being correct.

Neuro-Linguistic Programming

In the 1970s, linguists Richard Bandler and John Grinder at a California university stumbled upon a startling discovery. They theorized that not only do the words we use reflect our thoughts, but the words we use also shape our thoughts. Not all of what we speak is an end result; we listen to ourselves as well, and so when we say something, it reinforces what we've already said.

Let's consider an overweight person, who is obese not because of a medical condition, but simply through eating junk food and being a couch potato. If that person checks their weight, looks in the bathroom mirror, and says, "Look at me, I'm fat and ugly. I'll never lose this weight." Then that person has just shut themselves in the prison of their own negativity. Their prophecy will be self-fulfilling. They will continue to live a lifestyle of excess, thinking "What's the point, might as well enjoy it!"

If instead, that person were to say, "I've got to do something about this weight problem," they're on the right track, but that's still not good enough. Issuing a challenge to yourself sets yourself up for failure if you don't have the will-power to immediately follow through.

To cut to the chase, here are some more positive things our obese person can say:

- "What happens if I eat only salad today?" - Now there's no goal, no set-up for disappointment. Questions are always an invitation to discover. Doubtless, you can feel the difference if you eat fresh vegetables for one day. Just that little bit of feeling better can provide a confidence boost.

- "I might go for a walk." - "Baby steps," as they say. You're not making a resolution to jog five miles every day, because as soon as you miss a couple of days, you're defeated. A walk is a simple, fun recreation, and will leave you feeling different at the end of the day. It's a small improvement, but noticeable.
- "I'll try dieting today. I'll try to consume only 1500 calories today and see how close I can get." Again, you're not making ringing declarations to change the world forever. You're conducting an experiment. You can't fail when you perform an experiment; you'll find a result either way.
- "I'm starting to live like a healthy person." - After a few days on this slow road to progress, the confidence boost provides a massive headwind. It's exciting to make a change in your life and see the results! It encourages you to stay on the same track.
- "I'm becoming the person I always wanted to be." - After a week or two on the

treadmill and new diet, this is the positive self-reinforcement kicking in. When you define yourself as a "healthy person," you've stopped being the fat slob who lies around and eats their way into a coronary. No matter what shape you're in right now, showing that you're on the path to fixing yourself up immediately changes your identity.

Do you see the power of how we phrase things? The noted author George Orwell noticed the same tactic. In his novel "1984," he wrote of a dystopian government that controls the population, in part through the language. The language is called "Newspeak," and the purpose is to shape thoughts. The language literally has no vocabulary with which to criticize the government, for instance. Since our thoughts are shaped by the words we know, taking words away from your mind blocks off certain thought processes.

Also in the 1970s, Duke University's Psychology Department compiled a list of words which, in a neuro-linguistic sense, are "power words." These words get the most of your attention; they light up neurons in the brain. They are: Easy, Health, Save, Guarantee, Money, Discovery, Results, New, Love, Free, Proven, You.

Now, the next time you watch a television commercial, pay attention to the words they use. Something like: "Our healthy weight loss formula is based on a new discovery in medical research with proven results. Try our easy money-saving offer, and we'll send you a free sample - we guarantee you'll love it!" You'll be hard-pressed to find a commercial message that doesn't ring the majority of the words on this list.

Neuro-linguistic programmers - "brain hackers" if you will, recommend this method for getting people to agree with you:

- Build rapport by subtly copying whatever your target does. If they pace, you pace, if they scratch, you scratch. This is a subtle signal you send to their subconscious - see, we think alike. Remember our previous section in this book on body language.

- Begin by saying things that are very plainly obvious and require no effort to agree with. Try to speak their own thoughts out loud. Anything you can say, as long as it gets their head nodding in agreement with you, is a good step.

- Begin insinuating your own ideas into the conversation. Use smooth transitions here. Use words such as "because," "then," "likewise," "while," "as," "therefore," or "and so," to imply that the idea they agreed with leads them to your new idea.

- Guide this technique by watching their responses. If they reject your idea, back off and agree with them, then begin the pattern again, simply taking a different course of statements to arrive back at your original conclusion.

Here are a number of debate techniques which will work when practicing the above method:

- **Pacing** - With the step where you're mirroring your target's body language, try to adjust the tempo. See if you can speed the pace of your step to make them quicken their pace. If they do, you are now subtly in control. Cue them with a nose scratch or adjusting your legs while sitting and see if they copy that. If they do, you're the puppet-master now.

- **Normalization** - Got a radical idea? Start by proposing an even MORE radical idea. Children know this trick as "if you want a puppy, first ask your parents for a pony. Then when they say no, bargain for a puppy instead." This is a logic trap where you set somebody an outrageous limit, which they scoff at as being too extreme, and then you agree with them and propose a new limit that, by their own definition, is more reasonable.

- **Reframing** - This is the neuro-linguistic programmer's handiest tool. Anything can be reframed. You can reframe things all day long. Did your target reject your plan? Reframe it as a starting point and offer to negotiate to a compromise. Did they express distaste at your manipulation? Reframe it as their feelings in reaction - never "I'm sorry I said that," but "I'm sorry you feel that way about what I said." No matter how they disagree, reframe it as an agreement. Politicians are old hands at this trick.

- **Anchoring** - This is where you stick an idea into another one they already agree with, in our step where we insinuate our own ideas into things they already agree with. You love X, well Y is just like X, so you should love Y too. Advertisers anchor their breakfast cereal into the idea of a loving mom providing a healthy meal to their children, politicians anchor their plans for war in the idea of national defense, and a host of other professional influence workers do this every day.

As you can probably tell from our examples, the field of neuro-linguistic programming is a deep and fascinating science which is also a hot topic in many professions. Lawyers, who need to convince twelve jurors of an idea no matter how outlandish, practically have this school of study as their bread and butter. We cannot include all of it here, but be aware of the basics of the techniques as we've laid them out.

Take-aways:

- Learn to phrase sentences in a positive way that's beneficial to your cause.

- Influence people and subdue enemies by stealthily using 'power words'.

- Build rapport and use insinuation to 'hack' into your target's mind and get them to agree with you.

- Use the debate techniques to find an opening in whatever your current conflict is.

More Techniques Of Persuasion

It should come as no surprise to you that the Internet is a healthy arena where psychological warfare is developed and practiced. At the bottom rung is the common Internet troll, a person not at all invested in a current discussion who just makes posts to get a rise out of someone, then sit back and laugh as the angry flames pour in.

But just a notch above that is the loosely collected Internet group "Anonymous." This group has taken on everything from the Church of Scientology to politicians to businesses, with various results. What's notable is their adoption of the Guy Fawkes mask, popularized in the film "V For Vendetta." The mask, a bastardization of the face of Guy Fawkes, of British historic fame, is meant to intimidate and confuse. Anonymous members present themselves as an untraceable gang of Internet activists. While their small campaigns amount to little more than petty harassment, it goes to show that psychological warfare is at least effective in attracting attention.

A few rungs above this are the professionals. We will dive into each facet of the professional Internet opinion manipulator in subsequent chapters, but for now we'll skim over basic techniques of what is known as "astroturfing."

Astroturfing is so-called because it's "fake grass roots" support. A group of Internet forum posters with a paid agenda pose as random citizens and attach themselves to an issue, be it political or commercial, with an interest for their employer. Notable examples:

- Tobacco companies in 1993 created the "National Smokers Alliance," who drummed up an aggressive campaign of supposed outrage over tobacco regulation.

- Microsoft Corporation in 2001 created the "Americans for Technology Leadership" group, which spammed political and legal debates with support for Microsoft when the US government was prosecuting them for antitrust law violations.

- Just about every political campaign has employed astroturf to some extent. During the 2000 Bush-Gore primary election and Florida recount fiasco, several "rent a mobs" were hired to protest the recount of votes in Florida and demand that Bush be declared the winner.

- The presidential campaigns of Ron Paul (2008, 2012) and Bernie Sanders (2016) both employed a large sect of astroturfers to support their candidate. If the Internet is to be believed, both candidates had overwhelming landslide support and yet these high online polls failed to materialize into actual numbers at the primaries and caucuses.

It is the last example of Bernie Sanders that gives us an important leak: A document was circulated with specific instructions for manipulating online opinion in regards to the candidate. The techniques outlined in the document:

- **'Forum Sliding'** - Posting many irrelevant comments to bury an unfavorable comment.
- **'Consensus cracking'** - An intentionally false, unsubstantiated claim

is introduced, followed by increasingly strong support from a ring of apparently gullible posters who all side in to "believe" the posting and present stronger claims and evidence. Used to drive the casual reader to accept the conclusion.

- **'Topic dilution'** - Whenever a damaging post against the candidate is made, astroturf workers descend to sidetrack the discussion into dozens of irrelevant threads. Anybody who posts commenting on the topic is immediately attacked; the poster then goes on the defensive against the intentional trolling and the topic is diluted.

- **'Information collection'** - A false poster is brought forward to volunteer a controversial opinion and then ask who else holds that opinion. In fact, the original poster is a false flag, but everybody who posts agreeing with them will be carefully researched and noted.

- **'Anger trolling'** - General demoralizing of the other side's members. Trolling for trolling's sake, to make people who hold the opposite view become distracted and hopefully give up in disgust.

While all of these measures sound almost like a grade school classroom full of kids throwing spitballs, the techniques are in fact very well proven to work. In person, they may not be as effective - however, they are useful techniques to keep in mind should your psychological warfare mission take you to the online world.

Take-aways:

- Learn from the pros in shaping and dominating a debate or argument.
- Use the Internet to influence people or subdue enemies online, wherever possible. It's much easier in some cases!
- Exploit psychological tricks that online astroturfers use - You can still dilute a

topic or anger troll someone in real life, if it provides you with tactical advantage.

Case-Specific Examples

The Japanese have a saying: "Nothing is so costly as something given free of charge." You might not be surprised to know that doing a small favor for your target is a subtle way to get them to agree with you. However, it's equally efficient in reverse! Get your target to do a small favor for you, and then you get them to do a bigger favor.

Psychologists have tested this with subjects who were first offered a chance to do a small favor for someone, such as help change a tire, and then were asked their opinion on a controversial subject. Test subjects were more likely to agree with someone they had done a favor for already, than if they hadn't been obligated to help the person first. This is related to a powerful psychological quirk, the "sunk costs" fallacy. The brain rationalizes this as "I've already made friends with this person and I am invested in their well-being. Might as well go along with whatever else they want."

Salesmen practice all kinds of persuasion techniques - after all, they make their living off persuading others to buy their product. Some common sales techniques:

- **Setting a minimum** - Make the first step in committing to buy the easiest. Such as offering no money down on a car purchase.

- **Set a label** - A customer who has been told that they are a conscientious driver will be inspired to pay extra for a safer, more fuel-efficient vehicle. Here, you've given them a self-image to live up to.

- **False humility** - This is also known as "humble bragging." You admit to some incidental failing that has no impact on the sale and in fact makes the target trust you more. For instance, "admitting" that you can't resist giving a pretty woman a discount.

- **False exclusivity** - In this tactic, you pretend that your customer has to do something special to earn your sale as their reward. Night clubs have been doing this for years, which is why they have a velvet rope and a bouncer at the door to keep out the "riff raff."
- **Playing devil's advocate** - Psychological research has shown that people not fully committed to a position will reinforce their position when forced to question it. In other words, if your customer is only mildly thinking of making a sale, try to gently test their commitment by arguing them out of it - they will respond with increasing justification of their purchase until they insist on it right now. This is also known as "reverse psychology."

We hope this has been a powerful insight into the world of brain hacks you didn't know about. Perhaps even you, yourself, have been on the receiving end of some of these persuasion tactics. We'll dive into deeper and dirtier tricks in the next couple of chapters.

Take-aways:

- Learn from salesmen in persuading others to your bidding.
- To get somebody to do you a big favor, ask them for a small favor first.
- Make it easy for people to do your bidding.
- Use salesman tactics to sway people under your influence or subtly subdue your opponent.

Chapter 5: Winning the Battle of Wills

Before we move along to the darker arts of psychological warfare, we'll provide this section of intermediate psychological tactics. None of these are weapons-grade attacks, but all of them might serve in some situation or another.

Human nature is a fascinating thing. It can make people behave in apparently illogical ways, precisely because most people go through their day at half-throttle, not really paying much attention, thanks to their over-confidence in their own powers of reason and observation. It's easy to hit a "blind spot" where a person wasn't expecting the given tactic. The best inspiration to take for them is to remember the rule of "refuge in audacity" - the idea that something works because "nobody would be crazy enough to actually try that!"

Verbal Judo

Why do we call it "verbal judo"? Because it is for a defensive purpose. Judo is a self-defensive martial art, practiced strictly in a pacifist sense. Judo focuses on deflecting the enemy's attacks rather than meeting aggression with aggression. It is valuable whenever possible to practice this form of conflict negation. You win every fight you stop.

Approaches to verbal judo include:

- **Avoidance** - Recognizing a conflict early and heading it off before it becomes one.
- **Withdrawing** - Retreating on a position temporarily until a more advantageous time.
- **Deflecting** - Changing the topic or focus of a conflict.
- **Compromise** - Making a deal that's advantageous to both parties.

Speaking of fighting, ever watched a fight on soap operas? You've never seen such hostile, vitriolic lines delivered with all the inflection of reading a bus schedule. Two guys fighting on a soap opera: Both stand completely still, never raising their voices, six feet apart, not even frowning, just kind of scowling moodily, while the dialog is:

A: "I have found out your plan. And now I am going to work for the rest of my life to destroy everything you hoped and dreamed for.

B: "But you don't know about my ace in the hole. I still have Betty. I got her from you and I'm keeping her. And together, we will make your life a living hell."

A: "Oh, that's what you think you'll do. But that's not how the real world works. What's really going to happen is, my cousin Vinnie in the mob will be my agent on the side, who has been secretly brainwashing Betty without your knowledge. And together, we will reduce you to tears of agony and remorse."

It's like pro-wrestling kayfabe with all of the testosterone drained out. Well darn you, A. Darn you to heck, you bad person, you!

We've talked about a similar area before in this book, so we'll point you towards some further reading: "The Gentle Art of Verbal Self-Defense" by Suzette Haden Elgin, "Verbal Judo" by George Thompson, and "Verbal Self Defense for The Workplace" by Daniel Scott.

Take-aways:

- Subdue enemies with avoidance, withdrawal, deflection, or compromise.

- Adopt an attitude of Zen masters.
  Stopping a fight is the same thing as
  winning it.

Using Forbidden Fruit

Back last chapter, we talked about how one sales
tactic is to make your product apparently
exclusive. Offer a product to the public, and
there are lax sales. Claim your product is
exclusive to a select few customers, however, and
interest will spike. The psychology reasoning is
that people are attracted to having the most
freedom, so we see a lost opportunity as a
restriction. The laws of economics also show that
a product perceived as scarce immediately
becomes more valuable. It's a powerful method
of reverse psychology, and one that bears
mentioning for its notable examples:

- Agriculturalist and pharmacist introduced
  potatoes in France in the late 1700s. He

did this, not by simply offering them, but by planting a potato field and surrounding it with armed guards allegedly to spare the crop solely for the king's table. The guards were actually instructed to accept all bribes from the peasantry, who sure enough did do everything they could to get to the potatoes.

- Physicians for the British Royal Navy in the 18th century promoted healthy eating among sailors in a similar way. They advocated sauerkraut as a protection from scurvy, since it kept well and was rich in vitamin C. The problem was that its tart taste was unappealing to the British appetite. So they kept barrels of sauerkraut on board with signs saying "for officer's mess only!" Sure enough, the sailors soon regarded sauerkraut as a tasty and rare delicacy.

- Various countries in Europe, such as the Netherlands, have seen teenage marijuana usage drop from 11% to 8% since it was decriminalized. It's not forbidden, so it's not cool or rebellious anymore.

- "The Streisand Effect" is a notable variation. Actress Barbara Streisand forbid photographers from her wedding - so they hovered over her Malibu home in helicopters and took photos anyway. The resulting controversy attracted far more attention to an otherwise unremarkable wedding. Had she not called attention to it, it probably would have been a boring page-five story. As it is, it stands as the most notorious example of making something more popular by forbidding it.

- Notorious Wall Street scam artist Bernie Madoff pulled off the most daring version of this yet. When collecting funds for his gigantic Ponzi scheme, he would sometimes publicly turn down potential victims even if they begged him to take their money. This promoted the image that he was actually a savvy investor with a scare resource, as opposed to a common crook. He could also use the defense that he turned down money, since nobody could believe that a con artist would willingly turn away business.

Author Oscar Wilde once remarked that the surest way to sell a book was to ban it. This holds true for almost any form of media. Films, video games, books, music albums, and other products sell in far higher number if there's a controversy about their content.

Take-aways:

- Where applicable, use the illusion of 'forbidden fruit' to entice people into doing your will.

Exploiting Politeness

People are social creatures, and so they have a vulnerability to exploit. They do not want to be seen as rude, so they're more likely to comply with your plans if you can utilize their good manners in the bargain. Some notable examples:

- Japanese Zen master Dogen Zenji has a famous anecdote. An unruly student interrupted his lecture by saying that Zenji was not clever enough to control him. Zenji responded to the student "Stand up here so we may debate the issue." The student came up. "Stand over here so the other students can hear you better." The student shuffled over to the other side. Zenji reconsidered: "Come to think of it, why not take my podium so you can talk to all of us." The student did this as well. Zenji then thanked the student for following his control and told him he could sit back down.

- Various psychology studies show that simply supplying a reason along with a request makes the request more likely to be granted, even if the reason is ridiculous. Next time you need to cut in line at the copier, try asking "Can I cut in here? I just need to make a few copies." So does everyone else, but suddenly the fact that you've called attention to your own need makes it weigh more.

- In 1971, the Citizens' Commission to Investigate the FBI broke into the headquarters of the United States' COINTELPRO - run under J. Edgar Hoover's corrupt FBI - to swipe some documents exposing their practices which violated civil rights. How did they do this? They cased the building and found no access to the document room they needed. So they simply left a sign on a door saying "Please don't lock this door tonight." Sure enough, the night watchman left that door open.

- At least half of corporate espionage revolves around this tactic. Even if you're not authorized to be somewhere, you can hang around the door until somebody else comes through and then run to catch up -

they'll hold the door open for you. Employees will also be quick to open a door for you if you stand in front of it with your hands full of boxes.

Take-aways:

- Take advantage of people's natural desire to be polite while influencing them.
- Subdue enemies by exploiting their learned politeness. Force them to show themselves impolite to everyone in public if you don't get your way.
- Use people's desire to remain polite to influence them in doing what you want them to do, by making that the most polite response.

Being "Somebody Else's Problem"

"Somebody else's problem" is said to be some of the most beautiful three words in the English language. Whenever possible, when you can't avoid being spotted in more conventional ways, you can use the camouflage of authority combined with the appearance of knowing what you're doing to get into some very top-secret areas.

It's a very common trick: Walk around any business with a clipboard, hardhat, flashlight, ring of keys (they don't have to go to this particular building), or other tokens of job responsibility and pretend to be very wrapped up in a busy task. You will get doors held open for you, questions answered, access codes revealed, all with the eagerness to be helpful so typical of the average Joe at work.

Sure, some employees may wonder "What's this person doing here?" But they'll just shrug and go, " probably somebody else's problem."

The clipboard of authority - complimented by an official looking hat and blue collar uniform - is also great for getting almost anyone to follow your orders. Stand in a parking lot and direct people where to park, stand by a gate and charge admission, sit at a mall kiosk and accept orders. All you have to do is act like you belong there and nobody will question it.

In fact, many con artists, impostors, thieves, and crooks use tactics just like this to commit crimes all the time. Information like this is why we put the disclaimer at the front of the book.

Take-aways:

- Whenever possible, use stealth mode by disguising yourself as someone harmless and inconsequential.
- Use your body language and neuro-linguistic tricks to always appear to be someone else's responsibility besides the enemy you're trying to subdue.

Police Interrogation

Is it surprising that police and law enforcement officials in general use psychological warfare tactics in their line of work? Here, presented for your enlightenment, is the "Reid Technique" of police interrogation. The term "Reid technique" is a registered trademark of the firm John E. Reid and Associates, which offers training courses in the method. At the very least, this method is good to know in case of run-ins with the law, however incidental.

This is the most common method of interrogation, used by most law enforcement professionals in North America. If you're busted in the States, this is the process you will be put to.

Note that police first conduct a factual analysis of evidence, then an interview of witnesses, before your butt hits the chair in the interrogation room. So if they're grilling you hard, they either think that they have a partial conviction already but need your cooperation for a full conviction, or they have nothing unless you confess. If they already have enough evidence for a conviction in itself, interrogating you will be a mere formality, if it even happens at all.

Step 1: Confrontation.

They start by presenting the facts of the case and evidence against you. The "evidence" might be completely made up! There is typically some theatrics involved, as if your ultimate conviction for the crime is already a done deal. Detective enters with huge file folder (which may contain only a ream of blank paper), plops it on the table, flips through a few pages, looks at you while shaking his head. Boy, are you in trouble this time! We gotcha dead to rights, bub! We have it on tape. We have a file on you this thick! Your partner already ratted you out. We have three witnesses, one of them was a judge. And so on.

They'll look for signs of squirming on your part to confirm that they're on the right track. Actions speak louder than words.

Step 2: Theme development.

Forget getting the story out of you; first they'll tell you what they "know" happened. At this point, they will begin minimizing the crime, as if it's really a small matter, after all. They are offering you a chance to jump in and justify your actions, perhaps by blaming the victim; if you do, they'll be smiling and writing it down. If you instead try to deny it at this point, the next step is...

Step 3: Stop all denials.

Typically, you'll be interrupted with something like, "You'll get a chance to talk later, but right now you need to listen!" The goal here is to keep you from saying the magic "I didn't do it!" words, because getting the chance to say so will boost your confidence and make it tougher to sweat a confession out of you later. But see also...

Step 4: Overcome objections.

This is very different from a denial. An objection is an appeal to logic. "I couldn't have kicked that dog, because I have a dog and I love dogs and I'm a member of the ASPCA and PETA!" See the difference? As opposed to a denial, an objection on some basis of logical argument is actually a good sign that you're guilty as Hell and a liar with trousers ablaze. The detective will pounce on it with glee and say something like "Of course you love animals, which is why this one incident shows a temporary lapse in judgment in an otherwise fine, moral, upright citizen. Isn't that right?" No, don't nod your head here, dummy, you just CONFESSED to the lapse of judgment!

Step 5: Getting the suspect's trust.

"Boy, you must really be feeling the pressure now! You poor suspect, it must be tough being a habitual criminal, isn't it? Here, buddy, I'm really your friend. Heck, anybody can understand why you did it. The pressure got too much. You were drunk, and things got out of hand. The lazy lout had it coming. This time they pushed you too far. You were young and you needed the money. We understand. We're going to try to help you get through this." Look for physically closing in, invading your space, maybe offering you a sympathetic gesture, offer you a drink or a smoke, hinting that confessions sometimes lead to a lighter sentence. It's such a minor thing; why are you doing this to yourself when you could just give yourself up? Just tell us what happened; you'll feel so much better, and we want you to feel better because WE LOVE YOU! If you made it this far, why confess now and spoil the fun? We're only at number five, the show's just starting.

Step 6: Pouncing on defeat.

If you are, in fact, guilty, and you aren't a clinical psychopath, and you actually broke a real law that actually hurt somebody so you would feel bad about it, you should be breaking down at this point. They are watching you for the signs of a nervous breakdown: drooping head, tears of remorse, covering face with hands in shame, darting your beady eyes from one face to another in a silent plea for mercy, etc. A moment of silence will pass as the room holds its breath waiting for you to confess to the awful crime you've done. If you still won't talk, there's...

Step 7: The presentation of alternatives.

If you're still not cracking, a new phase of constructing a theme will start in earnest. There will be two or more scenarios presented, the difference being your motive to commit the crime. One of the ones presented will make you sound more innocent ("The dog pissed on you, so you booted it away."), one of them will sound more damning ("You are to dogs what Jeffery Dahmer was to little boys, and we'll be sure it says that on the sign over your electric chair!"). Those are your options. Those are your only options. So let me tell them to you again. Back and forth, back and forth, you're getting sleepy, guess it's better to confess to the lesser theory than it is to be convicted for the harder theory, better nod agreement when they say the "innocent" explanation next time... gotcha!

Step 8: You start singing.

Once they have even the tiniest sign of agreement or concession to any of the above methods, they will usually bring in another officer or detective or two. Confessions carry more weight in court if there are at least two witnesses, and the more, the merrier. Suddenly, there are these new people here who walked in smiling at you (they've been watching the whole thing from behind the two-way mirror), and they're all still smiling at you as you spill your guts to them, making you feel really lit up and happy... God, it feels so good to get it off your chest, and all these approving people suddenly showing up, hanging on your every word as you, the confessor, suddenly have the floor! Oh, what a happy ending, the interrogation will be over with soon! You almost expect the room to burst into applause when you're finished, but instead it's...

Step 9:

Writing it down, getting it on tape, sending you back to your cell, etc. Suddenly, you're back in a dark cage and back to being unhappy again... but detectives are poring over your every, meticulously-recorded word in preparation for your short trial and one of history's most amazingly long sentences.

That's the whole technique "by the book" anyway. Anything they do other than that is "off the book". And well it should be, because the psychological tricks to get information out of people who don't want to talk are barely scratched here. There's tons more techniques practiced by the boys in blue, and they're all legally practiced - unlike coercion and torture.

Take-aways:

- Use the interrogation script - tailored to your situation, of course - whenever you need information on someone.
- When it is advantageous, use the conversational tricks outlined in the Reid technique to trip your opponent into a confession. Getting a person to confess to a crime or trespass can be used for leverage against them.

The "Kansas City Shuffle"

The Kansas City Shuffle is the name of a class of cons so elegant that they're in a class by themselves. The basic element is that you have a target who knows there's a con going on... so you deliberately lead them to suspect the wrong con, while you successfully pull off the right one. It's a method of misdirection commonly practiced by stage magicians; for instance, showing "nothing up my sleeve" when the real trick is simple sleight-of-hand.

This is also a technique commonly used in warfare - real nation-to-nation combat that is.

- On D-Day during World War II, when the Allied forces landed at Normandy, they had managed to spread misinformation to convince Hitler that Normandy was just a diversion while the real intended invasion point was Calais - in fact, it was the other way around.

- Also during World War II was the British Operation Mincemeat. British intelligence planted fake documents and allowed them to be "caught." The documents led German intelligence to expect an invasion at Greece, so German forces moved defensive troops to Greece. The British invaded at Sicily.

The uses of propaganda and disinformation are so integral to international warfare that they'll get their own section later.

Kansas City Shuffle methods are so common that they're often a plot element in fiction as well. Dozens of heist and spy movies over the years, from the "Ocean's Eleven" series to the James Bond franchise, have illustrated it.

It's unlikely that the casual reader of this book will have access to the kinds of resources to pull off elaborate heists. But a smaller version can be used. For instance, if your target suspects you have a plot going, you can subtly lead them to guess the wrong plot.

From here, the going gets darker. Up until now, all of the techniques mentioned in this book have been of a borderline morality; you can justify them for moral or immoral purposes. However, the section we're about to plunge into is "Psychological Attacks," and being caught doing some of these can expose you to legal risks, so be advised.

Take-aways:

- Whenever somebody expects that you're using subtle trickery or conning them, give them a false target.
- Use misdirection to enhance your stealth mode - It's OK if people think you're up to something, as long as they have no idea of your real plans.

Chapter 6: Psychological Attacks

This is likely to be a challenging chapter. We'll be talking about levels of violence that are at least condemned by society, if not illegal, and some even against international law.

Those who scoff at the idea that psychological violence is serious need only consider such terms as "white torture." White torture is a non-physical form of torture practiced in prisons by some of the more barbaric countries on Earth - and by the United States in Guantanamo Bay, Cuba. It includes sensory deprivation, isolation, solitary confinement, threats against one's family, "white noise," being made to wear restricting clothes and to stand in stressful positions, sleep deprivation, loss of all privacy, and cutting the prisoner off from all information. Some confinements have prisoners in a cell too small to lie down in, under bright light and constant noise, never allowed to see a human face or hear a human voice, no clocks or windows to keep track of time, and being fed the minimum nutrients through a tube. Anybody who escapes such treatment is at least psychologically scarred for life, if not completely mad.

These practices are used because they dodge Geneva conventions and human rights laws, because they can't be proven as they leave no physical scars, and because guards are more likely to comply since these techniques aren't considered "real" torture. People often dismiss mental anguish because "it's all in your mind." But as these examples show will show you here, your mind is actually the worst place to get hit.

Another shockingly common practice is the use of white torture techniques in, of all places, "troubled teens" facilities. These are places such as teenage boot camps, religious boarding schools, and other organizations where teenagers with a criminal or disciplinary history (or whose parents are simply tired of taking care of them), get dropped off. In the name of "tough love," the kids end up subjected to all manner of white torture techniques, combined with peer pressure and group social violence. The children are encouraged to participate in each other's torment, such as encircling the victim and harassing them, and the effect is a cult-like atmosphere. Activists are working to tear down the legal protections these organizations have, but so far they're entrenched in the American juvenile system.

So, without further ado, here are a number of psychological attacks which can be applied in various contexts:

Gaslighting

Gaslighting is a form of mental abuse in which the victim is tricked into doubting their own sanity. Its name comes from the 1938 stage play "Gaslight" where a man slowly drives his wife insane just by disturbing her reality.

An example would be if a group of people in your home decided to take something of yours when you're not looking, then when you asked where it was, everyone would conspire to pretend as if it never existed and you were making it up. Or, you might decide to "haunt" somebody with a guilty conscience by making ghostly sound effects and "unexplained" startling events, to convince them that a ghost was haunting them.

Manipulative spouses and parents pull this kind of stunt with impunity. Some parents, intent on keeping a family secret, will do this to convince the child that they have false memories. For instance, a divorced parent with a new spouse might work to convince a young child that the new spouse had always been a member of the family.

For domestic abusers, all it takes is a pattern of twisting the truth. The abuser, after beating the victim, tells such excuses as "you made me do it," convincing the victim that the violence was their own fault. A consistent program of twisting the truth can play quite a number on a person who is helpless to escape the situation. It's the prime factor behind such effects as Stockholm Syndrome, where the victim declares an inseparable emotional bond to the attacker and swears to defend them. Some sociopaths who kidnap hostages can invoke Stockholm Syndrome in a matter of days.

Another technique of mental abuse is setting the victim up to fail. An abuser might give the victim a seemingly simple, but actual impossible task, such as doing all the laundry in one hour. But then they sabotage the washer so the clothes have to be cleaned by hand. The victim is then convinced that they failed and receives a "punishment" they have "earned."

It is also quite easy to gaslight someone innocently. In psychiatry, one example is the "Martha Mitchell Effect," in which a sane person's claims are chalked up by a mis-diagnosis as being the product of delusions or hallucinations. It's named after Martha Mitchell, wife of John Mitchell, Attorney-General in the Nixon administration, whose claims of White House officials engaging in a criminal conspiracy were first put off to paranoid delusions. Later when the infamous Watergate scandal broke the news, Mitchell was vindicated and was afterwards known as the "Cassandra of Watergate."

An even more handy example is the Asch Conformity Experiment, developed in the 1950s. This is very simple: You have a test room and multiple students. An elementary problem is put up on the chalkboard for the class to solve. Yet only one student is the actual test subject - the other students are actually part of the experiment. All of the planted students are to answer the problem out loud, giving the WRONG answer. The test subject will, more often than not, change their answer to conform to the group. There's nothing subtle about this: The problem can be as obvious as answering which of three lines is the longest. The answer can clearly be 'B' but if the other students all answered 'A', the test subject would reverse their answer to 'A' too.

In George Orwell's dystopian novel "Nineteen Eighty-Four," a prisoner of the oppressive government is tortured until he learns to "reason" that two plus two equals five. This is such a well-known example that "2+2=5" is now an Internet meme for forced institutionalized brainwashing.

Speaking of which, gaslighting is an important step in brainwashing. Since you're trying to change a person's whole frame of reality, it helps to break down their prior sense of reality first so you can rebuild them in your ideal.

You almost can't run out of variations on the theme of gaslighting. In fact, some form or another is employed whenever a person in authority leads those under them to a deliberately wrong conclusion. In the workplace, a boss may gaslight a secretary they don't like in order to try to force them to quit. In school, a group of student bullies may gang up on one student and gaslight the victim as just one more imaginative step in their campaign of torment. In the military, a drill sergeant may gaslight one private under his charge as a method of driving them to either shape up or quit. Anything you could qualify as "head games" can usually be classified as gaslighting.

Now, it is unlikely that the average individual has the resources to enact some elaborate campaign of slow psychological abuse complete with Gothic period atmosphere. But small change, casual incidents of shaping somebody else's reality can be pulled off with little preparation. The effect may not be lasting, but a pattern of cumulative effects over time, if carried out in a dedicated manner, can add up to the target having an increasingly slippery grasp on reality.

While gaslighting cannot actually induce proper mental illnesses, it can produce an effect similar to a delusional state.

Take-aways:

- Use your enemy's proneness to question their own reality to your advantage.
- Depend on people not paying close attention to gain the upper hand in situations.
- Wherever possible, use gaslighting logic to convince your enemy that the conflict was their fault, that you've just done them a favor, etc.
- Use "head games" sparingly, but surgically.

Catfishing

If gaslighting is the act of creating false events to fool someone, catfishing takes the extra step of creating a whole fake person! Catfishing is a more recent invention, named after a 2010 documentary film called "Catfish," in which a person is led astray by the creation of a fake persona.

Anyone who has used the Internet is familiar with catfishing. All it takes is the creation of a fake social media profile, through which you interact with someone else while convincing them that they're interacting with a real person. In other words, it's simply lying, but taking the extra step of creating a vast, elaborate system of lies to the point where you've fabricated an entire false life.

Online dating sites are positively riddled with catfishers, and most of them are scammers in third world countries. The scammer creates a fake profile and sends romantic come-ons through the dating network, enticing potential victims to get involved. Soon the "incidents" and "accidents" begin, in which the false profile was just about to meet with the victim, but had a flat tire or got kidnapped and needs the victim to send money to help them out. Various scams are conducted, then the profile abandoned, leaving a bewildered target wondering if there ever was such a person. Of course, there wasn't.

Catfishing is related to gaslighting in that it can be used for other purposes besides just scamming someone out of money. For example, a common technique with Internet trolls is to create several false "sock puppet" accounts, then bombard a target with many harassing messages from what appear to be numerous people. Coming from one target, attacks are easy to dismiss as "some nut harassing me," but when it looks like five people are telling you the same thing, you're more likely to retreat from the situation in confusion at least. If so, you've just been gaslighted, because the apparent "crowd" of peers all jeering at you has made you question your take on reality.

As we mentioned earlier about Internet astroturf, catfishing is also commonly deployed by companies, organizations, and other groups to push an agenda on the Internet. Except catfishing suggests a more involved, personal campaign.

Cyberbullying laws, in fact, are starting to recognize catfishing as a form of Internet harassment. One such law passed in some US jurisdictions in 2007 was inspired by the suicide of Megan Meier, a teenager who was driven to suicide by what turned out to be an adult woman who did not like her, and created fake social media accounts, including a false boyfriend, to harass Megan. This goes to show that games played with social media accounts can get dangerous very fast.

Catfishing is even used by law enforcement as a means of entrapping pedophiles. Vice cops create fake profiles for underage children and interact with chat rooms and message boards -

when they attract a pedophile attempting to meet the supposed minor for sexual encounters, the pedophile meets with a set of cuffs instead. Private detectives investigating spouses accused of cheating will sometimes create fake social media accounts for the same purpose of entrapping the target.

Once you're aware of how common catfishing is, it's hard not to be a little paranoid of online interactions. In fact, human nature and the law of averages indicate that you, the reader, have probably engaged in some form of online deception yourself, however innocently or playful, and know how easy it is. Don't worry, we know better than to assume everybody who clicks an "I'm over 18" button is legit!

Catfishing makes the Internet sound like a great evil. Should we blame this medium? If you think so, you're about to have your little moral panic theory blown to smithereens.

The Internet and video games are just media. Before both, people still actually found other ways to escape reality before the invention of home consumer electronic devices. Moral guardians complain that the Internet is a hotbed of lascivious desire, tempting our youth to sin. But porn existed as The Spice Channel when cable rolled out, nudie movie theaters before that, porn magazines before that, live nude girls performing behind smeary shatterproof glass before that, all the way back to cave paintings in Tassili n'Ajjer circa Neolithic era.

Before the Internet, people were engaging in socially nasty behavior and all manner of cons both long and short.

Every generation has had its "social ill," its media obsession and diversion that was acquired cheaply, practiced solo, and had a ring of moral guardians around it decrying that it was the end of humanity. There has never been a paradise of crystal spires and togas in the clouds where people were free from addictions and obsessively-pursued diversions. Humans, once they get the basic needs met at the bottom of the needs pyramid, become lotus eaters, one and all, no matter what's available. We've survived it before, we're surviving it now, we'll survive it in the future.

Of course, we have also always had our Professor Harold Hills and our Jack Thompsons and our Tipper Gores here to preach at us about the latest entertainment and how it's dooming us all to be hairy-palmed freaks - unless, of course, we save ourselves by buying their snake oil.

So we live in a world with Internet - use it wisely and defensively.

Take-aways:

- If it's advantageous in your situation, use catfishing over the Internet to create anonymous personas targeted at the person you're trying to influence or the enemy you're trying to subdue. It doesn't get any stealthier than that!

Propaganda

Our first two examples are all about the individual target, but propaganda is the same idea targeting the general public or at least a large target demographic.

Propaganda is a fascinating subject deserving at least half a semester of media studies to fully appreciate. But basically it's all about spreading lies or at least a biased version of the truth to twist and spin the facts to your liking.

All governments, in both war and peace, as well as all religions and all corporations, engage in propaganda of one kind or another. There are no exceptions. A few pages back we talked about Internet astroturf, which is related to propaganda in that it's the same intent to spread misinformation, but done covertly. Keep in mind that propaganda need not be false, just misleading or one-sided. The point is that it's intended to lead its audience into a certain opinion or frame of mind.

Government propaganda and especially during wartime has a long and well-documented history. World War II gave us a wealth of posters and other media. A unique asset of WWII propaganda was that even cartoons got involved, showing such familiar faces as Bugs Bunny and

Donald Duck defeating the Axis powers; these cartoons survive on YouTube replay indefinitely.

The aim of political wartime propaganda can vary. It can be aimed at the "home front," to galvanize the troops into action against the enemy. It can be targeted abroad, to make claims or state a case against the country's enemy. It can be aimed at discouraging alliances. Or it can be targeted directly at the enemy country. One common example is the US dropping leaflets over countries in conflict, which spread disinformation to demoralize troops.

Whether using propaganda in psychological warfare or defending against it, you should know that propaganda uses logical fallacies to make convincing claims. Here's a brief list of the more common logical fallacies used in wartime propaganda:

- **Ad hominem** - Attacking the target instead of what they do or say. Blaringly obvious in war posters that paint insulting caricatures of Mussolini and so on.

- **Appeal to accomplishment** - "We're all in this together!" Rousing the troops towards a goal. The aim is always a call to action.

- **Appeal to fear** - The enemy is always painted as a scary, immediate threat.

- **Moral high ground** - Of course, our side is always the side of justice and freedom, isn't it?

- **Misleading vividness** - Using garish and shocking depictions to oversell your case.

The full list of collected logical fallacies has grown so vast over the years that there's even a fallacy about being too concerned with fallacies out there, as lampooned in the Internet webcomic strip "Doomed to Obscurity" by Pete

Trbovich. So we can't list them all here. But propaganda with logical fallacies is also used in a non-war context, such as in advertising or high-profile media cases. An example is "cherry picking," when producers of certain products show a clinical test that shows their product to be more effective, while neglecting to mention the other trials where it failed.

On a personal level, propaganda is more properly called "gossip." Try it around your office, and you'll soon be caught. But if you're careful to insinuate small details into conversations, you can spread some interesting ideas around without anybody quite knowing how they got started.

Take-aways:

- Always give yourself and the people you want to influence "good press."

- Spread any untruth you want to be widely accepted. Do this ahead of time if it will come in handy.
- Use propaganda techniques of logical short-circuits to phrase debates. This helps to influence people most of the time.
- Study propaganda wherever you find it. Ask yourself, how is this intended to shape thoughts? How can I use the same technique?

Brainwashing

Brainwashing is the darkest and most damaging form of psychological domination. A brainwashed person is the puppet of their master, no longer a thinking person on their own.

Brainwashing is the technique of religious cults, many of which have proved to have disastrous results.

- The People's Temple cult of Jonestown, Guyana, in 1974 under the leadership of "Reverend" Jim Jones saw the mass suicide of over 900 people. All of these people were convinced to stand in line and drink poisoned drink mix, some even giving it to their babies in arms.

- In 1993, the Branch Davidians compound in Waco, Texas, had a bloody confrontation with an FBI standoff. In a reverse charge into their compound, already on fire, 80 members died rather than surrender.

- From 1994 to 1997, the Order of the Solar Temple attempted several global mass suicides, with 74 deaths falling on the dates around the equinoxes and solstices.

- In 1997, a California cult of UFO-worshiping web developers known as Heaven's Gate committed mass suicide, with all 39 members being found dead after being convinced by their leader that they would all be spirited away on a spaceship flying behind the comet Hale-Bopp.

All of which goes to show the lethal power of brainwashing. On a far more minor scale, some groups would argue that all childhood religious indoctrination is brainwashing. And some abusers or serial kidnap-rapists have gone to this length, claiming one victim at a time to keep as a virtual slave who was brainwashed using the Stockholm Syndrome effect into simply accepting their kidnapper as their partner in life.

Complete brainwashing and control of cult subjects follows a very rigorous pattern. There's a method established by all such persons:

- **Thought reform** - Fundamental changes to the way the target thinks. See earlier sections on propaganda, gaslighting, and such.

- **Isolation** - This is the most important factor. In order to control someone completely, you must cut them off from all outside influence. Frequently cult members are forbidden from watching TV or from communicating with their family.

- **Induced dependency** - Making the cult leader the sole source of livelihood. Cult members are forbidden from having their own money, and must live with the cult leader, only eating what they allow.

- **Dread** - Ruling through fear is the key tool of cult brainwashing. The cult leader convinces the members that there is a grave threat to them outside the cult compound. The cult leader also harshly punishes all disobedience.

- **Demands of dedication** - Finally, the cult members must pledge their lives, brain and blood, to the cause of the cult leader. They dedicate every waking hour to serving their leader's mission.

Keeping people in a cult is the ultimate in psychological warfare. It is also beyond the skillset of most people, which is a great blessing. However, brainwashing is a bit more common, but also far more involving than most people would undertake.

Fortunately, this is the end of our exploration. There is no higher level we can find.

Take-aways:

- Hopefully you never need to go this far!
- But learn from brainwasher's techniques anyway. It is all about controlling people, after all.

Conclusion

We hope you've enjoyed and been enlightened by our tour of the world of psychological warfare. You've learned some very dirty tricks and encountered some scary capabilities of mental combat, hopefully not to exploit the knowledge and become somebody we read about in the paper tomorrow.

Can psychological warfare be used for good? Certainly, as the section on police interrogation showed, it can be used to help capture criminals. If you believe your government is doing good, then using psychological tactics in the course of warfare is being used for good. If your greater cause is justified enough that removing the snoopy office clerk who is obstructing your plans is well worth the bother, then it's for the greater good. If it helped you win a fight with your child's school principle when they were being a typical obstructive bureaucrat, then that's a good thing.

Is psychological domination immoral? Besides justifying it - as long as you aren't leading a suicide cult or ruining someone's life, is it really so different from other forms of conflict? Certainly, you don't want to go around punching people, so if you got what you wanted with a kind word, that's certainly not outside of moral behavior. The worst people can say about you if you follow the methods and examples in this book is that you are manipulative. That's a character flaw, to be sure, but not one that CEOs, politicians, religious leaders, or even the occasional cat can't also be accused of.

That's why the skills in this book have to be applied with your conscience.

It is not our moral duty to withhold information just because it can be used to do wrong. Just as open information in the art of lock-picking helps the security industry know how to defeat a lock-picker, the open exposure of psychological manipulation tactics helps you become a stronger individual against the same tricks being used on yourself. The bad guys already have all of this information, rest assured.

Does psychological warfare always have to feel negative? NO! At the outset of this work, we outlined how simply being a sociable person who is well-liked is the best kind of psychological domination there is.

But a greater force than this book has already laid that groundwork for us. We owe a lot to Dale Carnegie's 1936 ground-breaking book, "How to Win Friends and Influence People." We cannot recommend Carnegie's original classic too highly - it has sold 15 million copies worldwide.

A second good read on interpersonal relations is Eric Berne's 1964 book, "Games People Play." It's a further, in-depth analysis of the kinds of one-on-one psychological combat people engage in their day to day lives, written by one of the first psychiatrists to think about the subject.

A third and final recommendation, which will seem an odd pitch, is Barbara Walters' book "How to Talk with Practically Anybody about Practically Anything." Walters is the same famous news anchor you know from ABC network's news program "20/20." Walters has interviewed everyone from all walks of life and shares great social tricks on conversation with them. Following her advice is also great help both for your social skills and to get a toe in the door towards influencing people without their knowing it.

If nothing else, this book should give you confidence in your day to day affairs. Remember, you don't have to go out and conquer the world or start an international conspiracy or be a master spy to be a good psychological warrior. You can just polish things off in your day to day life, having that little bit of an edge, that insight into what makes people tick and how they can be wound and where to look for the squeaky gears. Try those palm-reading tricks back in chapter one sometime. You can at least be the life of the party.

Don't be ambitious and try something you can't handle. Give it patience. Be the Zen master. Wait for the time to take seed. Psychological warfare is an art more than a science, so your gut will tell you when to make moves. Don't distrust your gut instinct: That's just your brain telling you something without bothering to explain the details to you.

Remember also that many people try these techniques, but don't know what they're called. Your co-worker might jockey with you while competing for your promotion. Your boss might be looking for a way to bypass you to promote his nephew over you. Your phone company customer service representative might be trying to pressure-sale you into a new data plan. But you'll be wise to all of it, if we've done our job at all.

We'll say again, thanks for sharing this time with us. And stay alert out there!